The Outer Banks

from a

Flying Machine

Martin Conway

Carabelle Books
Box 1611
Shepherdstown,WV 25443
Copyright© 1989 by Carabelle Publishers
ALL RIGHTS RESERVED
Library of Congress Catalog Number:89-60752
ISBN
0-938634-09-7
Printed in Hong Kong

Flying High

From the birthplace of man's first successful flight, it is especially fascinating to view the Outer Banks of North Carolina from the air in a flying machine.

This book is the result of such an adventure — to capture on film the villages, lighthouses and rugged, unspoiled beauty inherent in our national seashores, that together comprise the charm and mystique that make the Outer Banks the very special place it is today.

Most of the photographs were taken with my flying companions, Sue, Cara, and Andrew, in the fall of 1987 and throughout 1988 at an altitude of no more than 500 feet. The NASA photos were taken in 1970 at 60,000 feet.

We began by photographing the Corolla area on the northern extreme of the Banks. Working our way south we ended with pictures of the Cape Lookout-Beaufort area. Thus was *The Outer Banks From a Flying Machine* fashioned.

The project consisted of four flights of approximately twelve hours in the air and quite appropriately originated from the airstrip at the Wright Brothers National Memorial. And it proved great fun!

It is our hope that, as a visit to the Banks itself, this book will prove both enjoyable and provocative in knowing more of the rich history of this fascinating place.

The Magnificent Four

Pride of the Outer Banks

With the exception of the Ocracoke Lighthouse that was built in 1823, the four grand lighthouses of the Outer Banks were completed within 16 years of one another — 1859-1875.

The Cape Lookout Lighthouse was the first completed just prior to the Civil War. Not only did it have a nobility of its own, but it proved of such stunning dimension that it became the model for the three that followed including the lighthouses at Cape Hatteras, Bodie Island, and Currituck Beach.

The Light House Board, a Federal agency created to oversee the construction and operation of lighthouses, was primarily concerned with insuring that quality, both in materials and construction, would be followed in every detail. And with the passing of time the Board's insistence on excellence becomes increasingly evident.

Personifying the essence of the sea itself, these lighthouses stand as proud and distinguished as when built. They grace the Outer Banks in elegant simplicity and splendor. For, if nothing else, they are architectural gems that fascinate the eye and uplift the spirit by their commanding presence and exhilarating beauty.

Cape Lookout

Bodie Island

Cape Hatteras

Currituck Beach

Whalehead Club Mansion with Currituck Beach Lighthouse, standing watch together, grace the village of Corolla on the northern end of the Outer Banks. The mansion, completed in 1925 at a cost of $383,000, stands as an equisite tribute to women's rights and of a man's love for a woman.

Currituck Beach Lighthouse (facing page) at Corolla was completed in 1875. Unlike the other lighthouses on the Banks that were painted white with black identification markings, the Currituck Lighthouse was left unpainted as its mark of distinction to ships at sea.

The village of Duck was named for the abundance of migratory waterfowl that annually made Duck Sound (now called Currituck Sound) their winter home. What once was is now gone forever, the result of indiscriminate hunting and human encroachment. The community of Sandering (above), north of Duck, prides itself as the place with the beautifully restored U.S. Life Saving Station (buildings with flag).

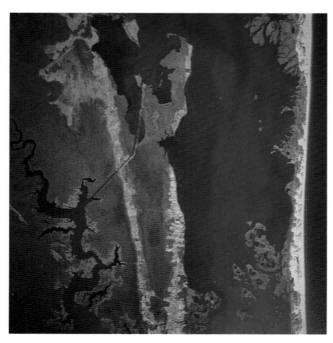

The pier north of the village of Duck (top) is part of the Coastal Engineering Research Center. The mission of this Federal agency is to control coastal erosion through a better understanding of waves, wind, tides, currents and coastal processes. Upon arrangements the center schedules tours for the general public and school groups.

A NASA photo (left) of Currituck Sound and the Corolla area from 12 miles high.

Kitty Hawk looking west from the sea to the Wright Brothers Memorial Bridge and beyond.

Highway 64 from Roanoke Island is a western point of entry to the Banks.

The three-mile Wright Brothers Memorial Bridge connects the mainland of North Carolina with the Outer Banks. It is the major point of entry for visitors to the Banks.

Kitty Hawk

Kill Devil Hill

Completed in 1872, the 150-foot high Bodie Island Lighthouse (left) is the third lighthouse to stand watch over this area of the Banks: poor construction destroyed the first; war the second. Whalebone Junction (top) at Nags Head looking north. The area in the foreground is approximately the site of Roanoke Inlet where Sir Walter Raleigh's early colonists left the sea to attempt settlement on Roanoke Island. Looking west (above) from the crossroads towards Roanoke Island.

Jockey Ridge State Park (top) in Nags Head is a towering, ever changing sand dune where gliding and hiking are popular recreational activities. Coquino Beach (below), south of Nags Head in Cape Hatteras National Seashore, is a popular bathing beach that includes beach houses, picnic shelters and life guard patrols. Nearby is displayed the remains of the ship-wrecked *Laura A. Barnes* that ran aground in a storm off Nags Head in 1921.

Cape Hatteras National Seashore (top right), the nation's first, was established in 1953. Under the management of the National Park Service, its 30,300 acres extend from Nags Head south of Ocracoke. Within the national seashore, nearly 6000 acres have been set aside exclusively for the care and protection of migratory waterfowl.

Pea Island National Wildlife Refuge (right) is managed by the U.S. Fish and Wildlife Service whose administrative buildings are near the site of the Pea Island Life Saving Station where the valiant all-black life saving crew was stationed.

The town of Manteo (facing page) on Roanoke Island. Its attractive waterfront on Shallowbag Bay features *Elizabeth II,* a replica of a 16th century ship used by early colonists. The state of North Carolina maintains a visitor center from where tours of the ship originate. Also near Manteo is the North Carolina Acquarium at Roanoke Island where a wide variety of fascinating maritime programs are offered to young and old alike.

Wanchese (top), on the south end of Roanoke Island, is a center for commercial fishing. But as the shifting sands of the Outer Banks continue to fill Oregon Inlet preventing seagoing fishing vessels from entering Wanchese, a way of life on the Banks is seriously threatened. Waterside Theatre (left) where the Roanoke Island Historical Association presents each July and August *The Lost Colony,* a symphonic drama.

The Herbert C. Bonner Bridge (left) opened in 1963 replaced the ferry service that had been operating there since 1924.

Oregon Inlet Fishing Center (below) is a concession operation of the National Park Service; it is owned and regulated by the Service, but leased to private management.

Wright Brothers National Memorial commemorates the site of the first sustained flight in a heavier-than-air flying machine. The time was December 17,1903. Authorized by Congress in 1927, the 431-acre site was transferred from the War Department to the National Park Service in 1933.

The Wright Memorial Monument was erected in 1931 by Congress as a tribute to Wilbur and Orville. It stands 61 feet above Kill Devil Hill, a stabilized sand dune from where the brothers experimented with gliders. The modern airstrip is a part of the national site.

Rodanthe (above), home of the famed Chicamacomico Life Saving Station, appears today much the same as it did in 1918 when the station's courageous Coast Guard crew entered a sea of flames to rescue 42 of the 52-man crew of the torpedoed British ship *Mirlo*. Nestled together just south of the Pea Island National Wildlife Refuge are the villages of Rodanthe, Waves and Salvo. They comprise the area once known by the grand Indian name, Chicamacomico.

Avon, formerly called Kinnakeet, was once a place of magnificent forests. Beginning in the early 1800's, wood from the trees was used for ship construction and Kinnakeet soon became known for its fine schooners. But as more trees were downed, sand dunes appeared in their place, increasing in size until the sand inundated everything in its path, including much of the remaining forests. Today little remains to indicate the rich abundance of trees and wildlife that was once Kinnakeet.

Cape Hatteras on a day in October. Surf fishermen, with their beach buggies fender to fender, compete for the rich abundance and variety of fish that the Cape offers.

Cape Hatteras Lighthouse completed in 1871, and distinguished from the other lighthouses, is 191-feet high, the tallest lighthouse in North America. It is also America's most famous, not only because of its stunning presence and prominent geographic location, but more recently by a national concern as to how best to save the structure from the ravages of an unforgiving sea that has advanced to within 150 feet of its foundation.

Upon the recommendation of the National Research Center, the National Park Service decided that when compelled it will move the venerable structure at a cost of approximately 4.6 million dollars that will take nearly a year. Moving the light will include first reinforcing the 28,000 ton lighthouse with pre-stressed rods and concrete tie beams. Next, huge lifting beams will be tunneled under the foundation and using hydraulic power the lighthouse will be lifted vertically and placed on rollers that will rest on steel rails supported by concrete ties. Finally, and ever so slowly, the upright lighthouse will be pulled by winches to its new site about 500 yards southwest from where it now stands.

It is interesting to note that when built the lighthouse was about a quarter mile from the sea. In 1936 the Coast Guard abandoned the lighthouse as the sea had advanced to within 50 feet of its foundation. At that point, the beach expanded, relieving for awhile, the threat from the sea. The following year the lighthouse was transferred to the care of the National Park Service; the Coast Guard continues to maintain its light.

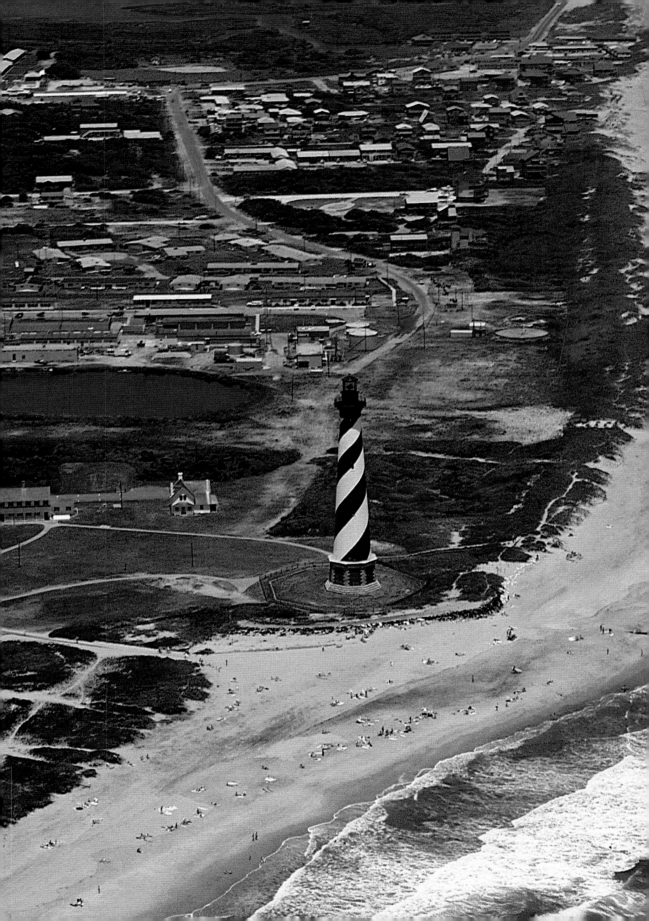

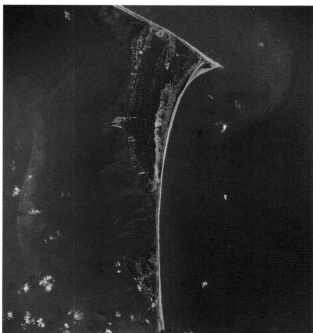

Frisco (above), formerly called Trent, was the site of a Union fortification during the Civil War. The lush forest of Buxton, in the distance, (top left) was once the home of the Hatteras Indians.

Cape Hatteras with its treacherous Diamond Shoals (shallow sand bars) that extend from the Cape about nine miles into the Atlantic. The shoals are kept relatively constant as they constitute the area where the warm waters of the Gulf Stream flowing from the south, collide with the colder, less powerful Labrador Current from the north.

Ocracoke Island

Hatteras Village

A visit to the Outer Banks would be incomplete without taking the refreshing 40 minute (14 mile) ferry ride across Hatteras Inlet. And it is free — courtesy state of North Carolina that has operated the service since 1954. Hatteras Inlet and Oregon Inlet further north were both formed from the hurricane that struck the Banks in 1846.

Ferry landings at Ocracoke Island and Hatteras Village (facing page).

Neat, picturesque Hatteras Village has been witness to its share of American history including a Union amphibious assault against two nearby Confederate forts, and in 1923 to the sight and roar of General Billy Mitchell's airplanes that were engaged in the famous demonstration to prove the value of airpower in modern warfare.

Due to its isolation, Ocracoke continues to retain an essence of its historic character. It is a rare and historically precious place where, especially for those who know its history, it possesses a maritime distinction and historical charm of its own. Here in 1718 the notorious pirate, Blackbeard, was killed in a stunning naval engagement by determined men of the British Navy.

Completed in 1823, the 65-foot high Ocracoke Lighthouse is the oldest operating lighthouse on the Outer Banks. It beautifully compliments the charm and character of the village. Its size and place in history almost assures that no modern structure will be allowed to mar its view nor intrude on its gentle presence. Overall, Ocracoke is a place with distinct echoes of a vanishing age, of dash and daring, a place where the feeling and spirit of things past prevails in the essence of the sea.

Established in 1753, Portsmouth Village, across the inlet from Ocracoke, was a thriving center for commerce and trade that lasted over a hundred years. In 1860 the village claimed a population of over 680 people. But as Ocracoke Inlet became increasingly shallow, thereby unsuited for seagoing vessels, Portmouth steadily declined. By 1930 only 104 hardy souls remained. With the establishment of Cape Lookout National Seashore in 1976, historic Portmouth was placed under the care of the National Park Service.

Beaufort, a lovely town of considerable nautical charm and historical character, is headquarters for Cape Lookout National Seashore. Under the management of the National Park Service, the seashore embraces a 55-mile stretch of undeveloped islands consisting of beaches, dunes, and marshes. Included within the seashore is the historic village of Portsmouth and the ever-impressive Cape Lookout Lighthouse.

Between Beaufort and the Outer Banks on Core Sound is Harkers Island (left) that from the air is an attractive, inviting place that merits a visit.

Completed in 1859, the 150-foot high Cape Lookout Lighthouse replaced the one built in 1812. Although the Lighthouse survived the war with minor damage, retreating Confederate forces did manage to extinguish its light. As the pride of Cape Lookout National Seashore, the lighthouse is entrusted to the care of the National Park Service with the Coast Guard continuing to maintain its light.

As with Cape Hatteras and its famous Diamond Shoals 70 miles to the north, Cape Lookout has its dangerous shoals that protrude about 10 miles out from the Cape. But Cape Lookout at its apex curves around to form an open bay, or bight, that for 300 years provided a safe refuge for ships at sea. Blackbeard and other pirates used the bight, and later British warships rendevouzed there during the American Revolution and the War of 1812. During the Civil War the Union Navy anchored in the bight, and during both World Wars I and II, it was a principle gathering place for European-bound convoys. Today it serves as a haven for small recreational craft.